I Can Paste!

An imprint of Carson-Dellosa Publishing LLC
Greensboro, North Carolina

Brighter Child®
An imprint of Carson-Dellosa Publishing LLC
P.O. Box 35665
Greensboro, NC 27425 USA

All rights reserved.   ISBN 0-7696-5372-3
Cover printed in Hagerstown, MD U.S.A.
Interior printed in Marceline, MO U.S.A.

040117791
056117810

7 8 9 10 11 WAL 15 14 13 12 11

Table of Contents

The Importance of Fine Motor Skills

Welcome to *Big Skills for Little Hands: I Can Paste!* This hands-on activity book is an introduction to pasting skills. The act of pasting and manipulating small objects will help your child develop fine motor skills. Fine motor skills are movements or activities that are produced by small muscles or muscle groups. Children in preschool spend a lot of their day developing these muscles in their hands. Developed motor skills are the key to success in school.

Developing fine motor skills is also an important part of brain development. Movement helps the organization of the brain. It reinforces growth and builds connections between different parts of the brain. More connections mean more brain power!

Fine motor skills are essential to developing the coordination, hand strength, and brain power needed to write, cut, button, zip, and eventually read. Finger plays, turning pages in books, screwing lids on and off jars, hammering nails, molding dough, sorting, pouring, and building with blocks are all examples of fine motor activities. These play experiences also develop dexterity, strength, eye-hand coordination, and visual discrimination.

Arts and crafts are a great way to enhance your child's fine motor skills. Not only are your child's little fingers bending, twisting, pinching, and pulling, they are also engaged in color, texture, and a variety of crafting mediums. The activities in this book are specifically structured to address your child's growing fine motor skills. There are parent instructions and tips on each page to guide you as you work through this book with your child. Remove each page from the book before your child begins working on it. Then, separate the activity section from the directions by cutting along the solid line. Please refer to pages 197–200 for additional activities you can do at home to enhance your child's fine motor abilities.

Save your child's creations in a shoebox that he or she decorated. Your child can use them later for play or arts and crafts. Enjoy working through this book with your child. The time you invest in your child's development is priceless and will reap countless rewards for years to come!

Glue and Safety

Using Glue

This book was designed to be completed with the child and parent working together to maximize learning opportunities. You will be responsible for cutting out the parts that your child will be gluing. Take time to cut carefully along the line so he or she will have a greater opportunity match the cut section to its proper location on the activity page. Encourage your child to do a "dry run" and place the section to be glued in the proper spot before applying the glue. That way he or she can see where it goes and move it around before working with the adhesive.

Squeezing a glue bottle can be tricky and frustrating. You can help alleviate this frustration by placing a quarter-size portion of glue on a paper plate. Have your child dip his or her finger in the glue and then spread it on the item to be glued. If your child is hesitant to touch the glue, allow him or her to use a paintbrush, cotton ball, or a cotton swab to apply the glue. Glue sticks are also good alternatives to white glue. If your child has trouble seeing where he or she applied the glue, you can purchase colored glue or add a few drops of food coloring to the glue you already have. Visit your local craft store. Many carry a wide selection of glues in a variety of applicators.

You can model holding the paper down with one hand as you spread the glue on the paper using the index finger on your other hand. You can hold the paper down for your child until he or she can do this independently. As you should with all new tasks you introduce to your child, offer a lot of encouragement. Do not expect your child to do it perfectly on the first attempt.

Try completing a couple pages a day with your child. There may be times when your child wants to do more than two or three activity pages a day. In those cases, give your child plain scraps of paper and let him or her practice gluing the scraps on to a larger sheet of paper. You can also refer to the extension activities in the back of the book.

Safety First

Many parents are wary of letting their young children use glue. They worry about their child's safety, and they also worry about the mess. The white glues available today are non-toxic and safe for use. But, if you prefer, you can make homemade glue using this recipe:

- 3/4 cup water
- 2 tablespoons corn syrup
- 1 teaspoon white vinegar
- Small saucepan

- Small bowl
- 2 tablespoons cornstarch
- 3/4 cup cold water

Directions:
1. Mix the water, corn syrup, and vinegar in the saucepan.
2. Bring the mixture to a rolling boil.
3. In the small bowl, mix the cornstarch with the cold water.
4. Add this mixture to the hot mixture slowly. Stir until the mixture returns to a boil.
5. Boil for one additional minute before removing from heat.
6. Cool.
7. Pour into an airtight container and let stand overnight before using.

Even though most glue brands are not hazardous, it is best to store glue out of your child's reach. Keep the glue on the top shelf of a cabinet or in a drawer with a safety lock on it.

To avoid a mess, provide your child with a smock (an old button-down shirt will do) and a wet rag. Encourage your child to wipe his or her hands off on the wet rag after each activity.

Brain Research and Kindergarten Screening Guide

What Brain Research Reveals

The first five years of life are a period of unparalleled growth in all areas of your child's development. It is in these years that children develop the basic knowledge, understandings, and interests they need to reach the goal of being successful learners.

Recent research about how quickly children's brains grow and develop emphasizes the importance of getting your child off to a good start. Thanks to such neuroscience tools as PET, MRI, CAT, and Ultrasound, scientists have learned about the structure of the brain and its capabilities.

At birth, a child has over a hundred billion brain cells. By age three, hundreds of trillions of synapses (connections among those cells) have developed in the brain. These synapses form a complex control center for making sense of the world—not only to see, hear, move, taste, and touch, but also to think, feel, and behave in particular ways. In other words, a preschooler's brain is vastly more active and complex than was previously known!

The brain's synaptic control center is constantly making sense out of many bits of information. It compiles data from many sources to determine patterns in formation, such as size, color, movement, etc. Once a pattern is detected and established, the brain "stores" it in its memory.

Even though genes determine how your child's brain is wired, it is your child's environment that determines his or her brain's sophistication. Brain research also reveals that experiences connected to *EMOTION*, such as laughter, are more easily remembered.

Memory is also enhanced when people are under stress. Positive *STRESS*, such as excitement or anticipation, causes the body to release adrenaline. Negative stress, such as worry or anxiety, causes the release of cortisol. Both chemicals act as a kind of "memory glue."

Researchers have discovered that certain *SCENTS* can trigger the ability to create and think. For example, cinnamon, peppermint, and lemon promote mental alertness; whereas orange, rose, and lavender are linked to calm relaxation.

COLOR stimulates your child's brain as well by releasing natural chemicals that affect his or her mood. Certain colors, such as blue and green, promote a sense of calm tranquility and peacefulness. Red and yellow encourage energy and creativity. Neutral colors, such as beige and off-white, instill a sense of self-confidence.

Research reveals that the brain functions in rhythmic cycles according to the release of hormones during periods of **_SLEEP_** and alertness. Consequently, your child's short-term memory is most efficient in the morning, and long-term memory reaches peak efficiency in the afternoon.

Your child's brain also benefits from regular **_EXERCISE_**. The increased flow of blood and oxygen to the brain results in improved short-term memory and an ability to react more quickly due to the release of adrenaline and endorphins. Exercise also causes your child to engage both the left and right sides of the brain, stimulating both creativity and logical thought at the same time.

What Parents Can Do

Since the biggest window for learning happens by age five, children's experiences during this window determine what they learn. Although play sounds simple, it is your child's classroom!

 for experiences associated with emotions and the five senses:

- Add peppermint or lemon extract or orange-flavored drink-mix crystals to your child's finger paint; offer scented markers for drawing and coloring activities; make potpourri from cinnamon sticks, cloves, and dried lavender and rose petals.
- Use reds and yellows to stimulate creativity when your child is playing make-believe, building with blocks, or doing artwork.
- Offer a variety of textured objects for your child to sort according to texture, shape, or size, such as foam packing peanuts, feathers, strips of satin and fur, wooden blocks, pieces of sand paper, clothespins, etc.
- Encourage your child to make as many alphabet letters as possible using just his or her body.
- Encourage your child to be silly by wearing clothes backward or pretending to be a favorite animal.
- Sing throughout the day with your child; clap and dance to music; make or buy simple musical instruments to play, such as cymbals, drums, whistles, horns, kazoos, etc.
- Use facial expressions to represent different moods for your child to identify; act out simple charades, such as a birthday party; play Follow the Leader or Simon Says.

Language stimulation has been proven to make the most dramatic difference in brain development between infancy & early elementary school years. Engage your child early—talk, read, listen, sing—about people, things, and activities that are familiar, important, and interesting.

 TIPS for experiences associated with language development:

- Help your child remember his or her phone number by setting it to a familiar song, such as "Twinkle, Twinkle, Little Star."
- Have your child help you describe the emotions involved in celebrating a birthday or holiday.
- Encourage your child to create a snack or dinner menu and pretend to be a restaurant server and/or customer.
- Invent your own "Knock-Knock" jokes and tongue-twisters.
- Have your child describe what his or her dinner looks, smells, and tastes like, or what clothes should be worn for different seasons and times of the day.
- Allow your child to record his or her own story or message on a tape recorder.
- Encourage your child to invent rules for parents to follow; act out a typical bedtime routine in role reversal with your child as parent and you as child; have your child stage a pretend play using puppets.
- Have your child retell a favorite story for you to listen to.

Fine-motor activities exercise your child's finger muscles stimulate brain growth.

 TIPS for experiences associated with exercise and coordination:

- Play with pegs, play dough, lacing boards, stringing beads, puzzles, and other manipulatives.
- Have your child do finger plays, such as "Where Is Thumbkin" and "Itsy-Bitsy Spider" with you often.
- Take advantage of frequent opportunities for your child to use scissors properly, such as cutting out newspaper coupons or shapes drawn on paper.
- Provide eyedroppers, sponges, measuring spoons, and basters for your child to use during water play activities.
- Provide tweezers or clothespins for your child to use to pick up and transfer small items, such as dried beans and buttons, from one place to another.
- Have your child use his or her fingers as a bubble wand through which to blow bubbles.
- Invite your child to help you shuck corn on the cob or shell peanuts.

Large-motor and cross-lateral activities exercise your child's brain by increasing the flow of blood and oxygen and stimulating cross-over learning.

 for experiences associated with exercise and coordination:

- Play action games, such as Simon Says, Red Light–Green Light, Hokey-Pokey, or Follow the Leader.
- Invite your child to walk like a crab or monkey or elephant, or to pretend to be an alligator using his or her arms as the jaws.
- Teach your child simple dances, such as the Twist, the waltz, or the polka.
- Make up hand jives with your child, slapping right hands to left knees, etc.
- Invite your child to walk on a balance beam or a long strip of masking tape.

Preschoolers are especially interested in knowing how things work. This curiosity is natural motivation for developing strategy and problem-solving skills.

 for experiences associated with problem-solving and analytic thinking:

- Encourage your child to find things in patterns, such as repeating colors in a rug or blanket.

- Ask your child how to solve child-sized problems, such as what to do when juice spills on the floor or when a light burns out.
- Teach your child riddles and introduce brain teasers, such as "I'm thinking of a vegetable that's green."
- When reading stories that present problems, such as The Three Billy Goats Gruff, ask your child to predict what might happen or to decide what is real and what is make believe.
- Ask "what if" questions, such as "What if apples were the only food?" or "What if horses could talk?" or "What if it never rained?"
- Provide opportunities for your child to compare and contrast activities, stories, and objects.
- Encourage your child to brainstorm a different ending to a familiar story.

Kindergarten Readiness Screening

When parents think about kindergarten readiness, they sometimes focus too much on academics. The skills that define readiness are far broader than knowing letters, numbers, and colors. To be ready for kindergarten, your child needs to have a positive attitude toward starting school and to be receptive to learning new things and making new friends.

The best way to learn what will be expected of your child is to contact the school your child will attend and speak to the teachers there. If a kindergarten readiness screening will be offered, take advantage of it.

Kindergarten readiness screening provides readiness feedback for parents who want their child to have the best possible start when entering kindergarten. It helps the kindergarten staff get an idea of the developmental level of each child before the year actually begins, so appropriate planning and instruction is in place for the incoming class. At the same time, it provides each child with a low-key, non-threatening opportunity to sample some fun, play-based activities in a comfortable school atmosphere.

Typically, kindergarten staff and other school aides set up several different activity stations in a room for your child to visit. Depending on the size of the staff and the room, the activities may accommodate one child at a time or small groups.

The following areas of development reflect the most recent national prekindergarten guidelines for children who are kindergarten bound. Supporting each area of development are some examples of typical kindergarten screening observations and activities.

Self-Help and Social Skills

In kindergarten, young children will need to work well in large groups, get along with new adults and other children, and share the teacher's attention with other youngsters. Classroom routines will also be different from children's at-home routines. Consequently, children need to be:

- Able to be away from parents or people they know for a few hours without being upset.
- Willing and happy to be going to school.
- Able to listen attentively when spoken to for three or more minutes.
- Willing to try new tasks, and to try them again if they don't succeed the first time.
- Able to follow a two- or three-step direction, such as "Close the door and hang up your coat."

- Able to play with other children without having a lot of fights.
- Able to do some self-help things for themselves, such as take off and put on jackets and sweaters.

Speech, Language, and Hearing Development

It is very important for a child entering kindergarten to be able to understand his or her teachers in order to learn and to know what to do. Likewise, it's very important for a child to be able to speak clearly and to be understood by others in order to express his or her needs. In addition to identifying any speech and hearing disorders, most kindergarten screenings also assess the following language developments:

- speak clearly enough so that people other than child's own family and friends can understand easily
- repeat a simple sentence
- respond to simple directions, such as where to sit or throw a ball
- talk in complete sentences of five to six words
- produce early-developing initial and final consonant sounds—*n, m, p, b, h, k, g, f, w, y, t, d*
- begin to produce later-developing sounds—*s, z, l, r, sh, ch*
- look at pictures and then tell stories about them

Large-Motor Development

Before going to school, children need to have good control over their movements. They need to be able to sit, stand, walk, climb stairs, and run without bumping into things, hurting themselves, or breaking things. In school, they'll be part of a group that is doing the following things:

- walk down steps placing one foot on each step
- walk forward on a line putting one foot after the other
- walk backwards for six or seven steps without turning to look behind
- stand on two feet with hands on hips, and bend body forward, backward, and sideways
- hop with two feet together
- hop on one foot a few times without falling
- jump using both feet at the same time

- kick a ball
- pump himself or herself on a swing
- balance on one foot for a few seconds
- run without falling frequently
- bounce a ball five consecutive times
- bounce a ball to another person 4 or 5 feet away
- throw and catch a ball using both hands
- carry something on top of something else, such as a juice box on a tray
- touch parts of his or her body with both hands, such as shoulders, neck, knees, toes, hips, chest
- dance while moving forward, backward, sideways left, and sideways right
- skip
- clap hands to music

Fine-Motor Development

In school, children need to use their hands and fingers to open, close, and hold things without dropping, breaking, or spilling them. They need to be able to hold pencils and crayons correctly so they can learn to write and do math. The following tasks allow for fine-motor skill development:

- hold a pencil or marker comfortably using thumb and fingers
- open a door using a doorknob
- use crayons without breaking them
- use round-tipped scissors effectively
- color and stay within lines reasonably well
- copy a square on paper
- draw a reasonably good circle on paper
- put together a 9-piece puzzle
- print first name using capital and lowercase letters
- use paste or glue without too much mess
- string wooden beads together
- hammer pegs on a board
- use a spoon without spilling
- get a drink of water without a mess
- turn pages of a book without tearing pages

General Knowledge

There are some general things children need to know so they will understand what's going on around them and what teachers and others are talking about:

- know their own name, age, sex, address or street name, and phone number
- know mother's and father's first and last names
- know names and ages of brothers and sisters
- name several parts of their own body, such as *nose, mouth, hair, eyes, legs*
- name some things that are around their home, such as *bed, door, steps, table*
- know some words for when things happen in time, such as *now, later, soon, never, before bedtime*
- know words for how things compare, such as *same, different, more, less*
- know something about the places around them and what happens there, such as *store, gas station, school, doctor's office*
- know appropriate words to use to ask to go to the bathroom

Academic Readiness Components

A kindergarten-bound child will also benefit from knowing some pre-academic concepts:

- understand basic concepts
  - positions and locations, such as *top, middle, bottom, left, right, down, up, below, across, over*
  - quantity, such as *less, more, many, few, heavy, light, small, large*
  - recognize feelings, such as *happiness, sadness, anger, fear*
- demonstrate some memory perception
  - can identify which object was removed from an earlier group
  - can match objects to pictures
- demonstrate strategies for understanding concepts
  - understand simple cause and effect, such as the idea that touching something hot can cause a burn
  - can sort objects into categories, such as *vegetables* are food
  - can identify and name the capital letters of the alphabet

- can identify concepts about print, such as recognizing the cover of a book and understanding that words read from left to right
- understand the difference between letters and numerals
- can briefly retell a story he or she has just heard
- can describe what he or she is playing
- can describe his or her drawing
- know some nursery rhymes
- can state choices about clothing
- can follow directions for simple games, such as Simon Says!
- ask questions beginning with *why* or *how*
- recognize his or her own name in print
- make actual letters, such as those in his or her name
- attempt to print other letters and some words

ACTIVITY 6
Berry Time

Directions: Your child will practice placing objects on a specific spot on the page. Cut the berries from the bottom of the page. Have your child paste the berries somewhere on the plant. This activity presents a good opportunity to practice counting, review colors, and discuss healthy eating habits!

Place objects on a specific spot on the page.

Adult, please cut out the strawberries.

ACTIVITY 7

Apple Tree

Directions: Your child will practice placing objects on a specific spot on the page. Cut the apples from the bottom of the page and count them with your child. Then, have your child glue the apples on the tree. In this activity, your child will still be pasting objects randomly, just within the boundaries of the apple tree.

Place objects on a specific spot on the page.

Adult, please cut out the apples.

ACTIVITY 8

Spot the Dog

Directions: Your child will practice placing objects on a specific spot on the page. Spot lost his spots! Can your child help Spot put his spots back on? Cut the spots from the bottom of the page and have your child paste the spots on the dog. Your child can practice confining the spots to the dog by arranging them on the page prior to pasting.

Place objects on a specific spot on the page.

Adult, please cut out the spots.

On Top of Spaghetti

Directions: Your child will practice placing objects on a specific spot on the page. Cut out the meatballs at the bottom of the page and count them with your child. Then, your child will put the meatballs on the spaghetti to make a delicious dinner!

Place objects on a specific spot on the page.

Adult, please cut out the meatballs.

ACTIVITY
11

Circus Seal

Directions: Your child will practice placing objects on a specific spot on the page. Cut the ball from the bottom of the page and have your child paste it on the seal's nose. Placing an object on a specific spot takes more concentration and precision than the previous activities. Be patient and encouraging! It is okay if your child does not place the ball exactly on the seal's nose. Your child can practice by placing the ball on the seal's nose before he or she tries pasting it.

Place object on a specific spot on the page.

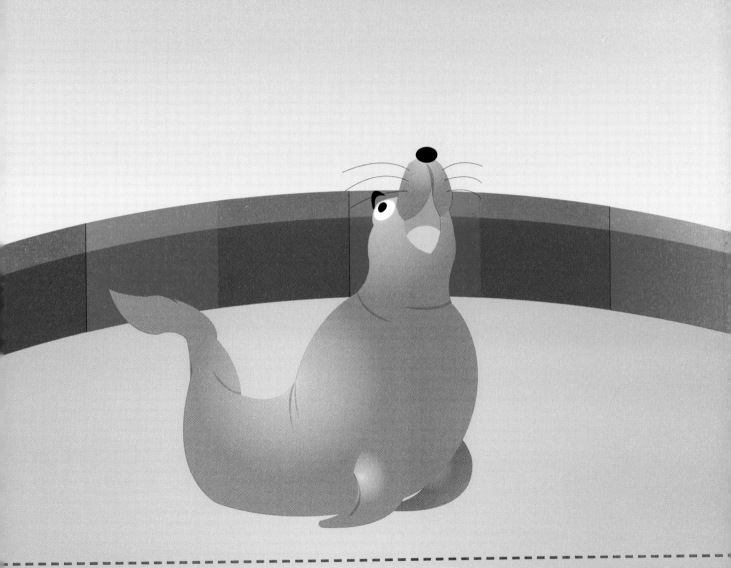

Adult, please cut out the ball.

Flower Garden

Directions: Your child will practice placing objects on a specific spot on the page. Cut the flowers from the bottom of the page and count them with your child. Then, have your child glue the flowers on the stems.

Place objects on a specific spot on the page.

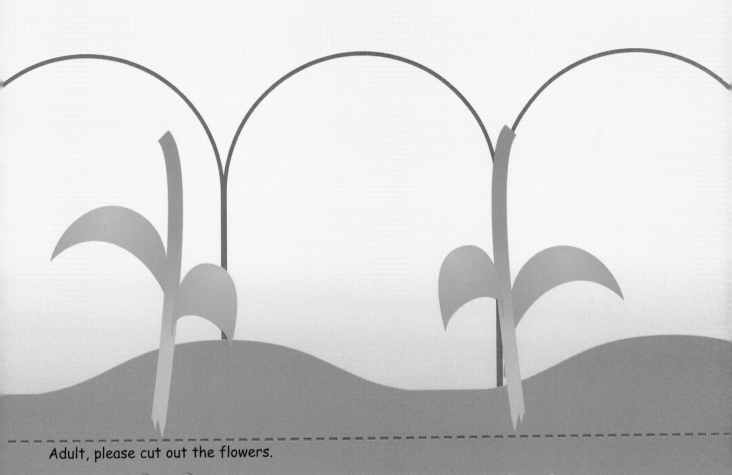

Adult, please cut out the flowers.

Funny Farm

Directions: Your child will practice pasting pieces together to finish a puzzle. Your child will glue the pieces down to make a picture. Can he or she find five funny things about this picture?

Paste pieces together to finish the puzzle.

Adult, please cut out the pieces.

ACTIVITY 16

Eggs in a Nest

Directions: Your child will practice placing objects on a specific spot on the page. Cut the eggs from the bottom of the page. Then, have your child paste the eggs in the nest.

Place objects on a specific spot on the page.

Adult, please cut out the eggs.

ACTIVITY 17
Giant Giraffe

Directions: Your child will practice placing objects on a specific spot on the page. Cut the spots from the side of the page. Then, have your child paste the spots on the giraffe. This is a good opportunity to practice counting!

Place objects on a specific spot on the page.

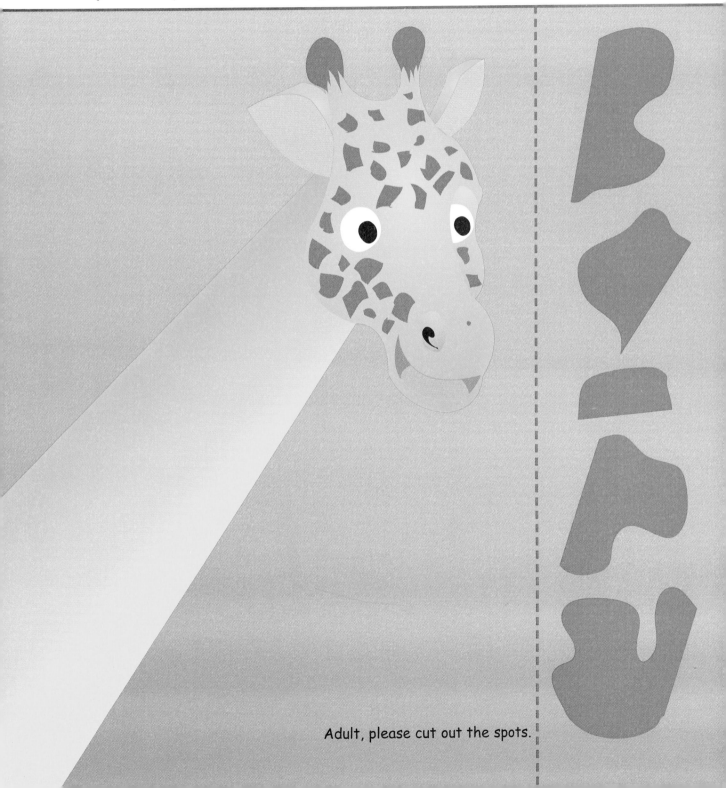

Adult, please cut out the spots.

ACTIVITY 18

Frog's Balloons

Directions: Your child will practice placing objects on a specific spot on the page. Cut the balloons from the bottom of the page. Then, have your child paste the balloons on the strings. At this point, your child should be more skilled placing the balloons in the correct spot. Take this opportunity to review colors with your child. Can he or she name the color of each balloon?

Place objects on a specific spot on the page.

Adult, please cut out the balloons.

ACTIVITY 19

Park the Cars

Directions: Your child will practice placing objects on a specific spot on the page. Cut the cars from the bottom of the page. Then, have your child "park" each car in an open parking space.

Place objects on a specific spot on the page.

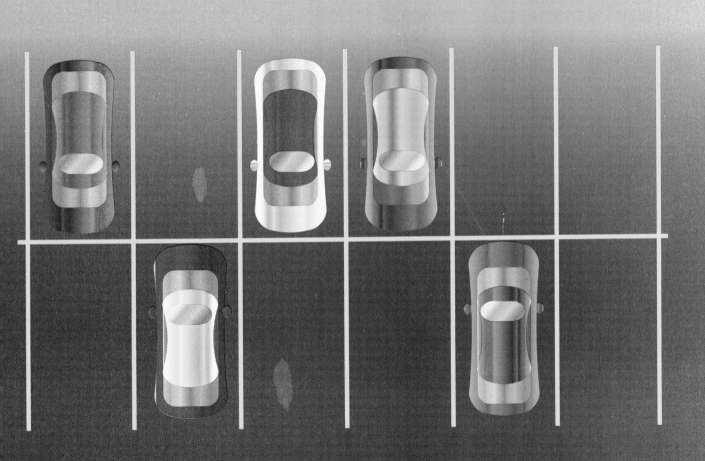

Adult, please cut out the cars.

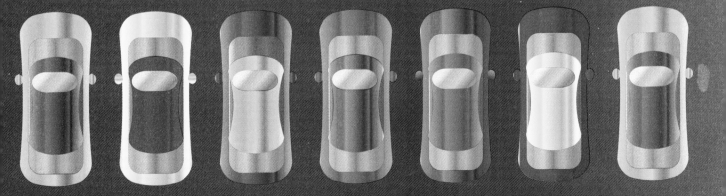

ACTIVITY 20

Bear's Buttons

Directions: Your child will practice placing objects on specific spots on the page. Cut the buttons from the side of the page. Then, have your child paste each button on top of a black dot on the bear's vest. This activity involves more hand control for more precise placement. Encourage your child to practice placing the buttons on the dots before he or she begins pasting.

Place objects on specific spots on the page.

Adult, please cut out the buttons.

Rise and Shine

Directions: Your child will practice placing objects on specific spots on the page. Cut the sunshine rays from the bottom of the page. Then, have your child paste them on the black dots around the sun.

Place objects on specific spots on the page.

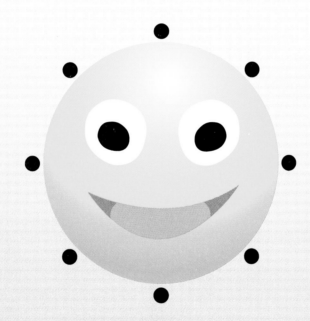

Adult, please cut out the rays of sunshine.

Pepperoni Please

Directions: Your child will practice placing objects on specific spots on the page. Cut the pepperoni from the bottom of the page. Then, have your child paste the pepperoni on the pizza so they cover up the black dots. Cut the pizza in half and use it to demonstrate the concept of *part and whole*. Introduce these new words as you cut.

Place objects on specific spots on the page.

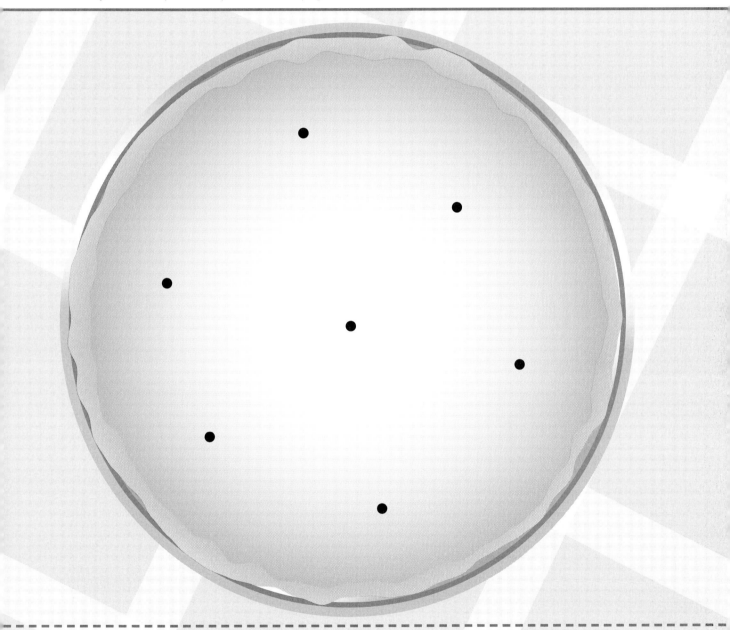

Adult, please cut out the pepperoni.

Beach Day Puzzle

Directions: Your child will practice pasting pieces together to finish a puzzle. Cut out the puzzle pieces for your child. He or she will arrange the pieces of the puzzle to make a picture and then paste them on the page.

Paste pieces together to finish a puzzle.

Adult, please cut out the pieces.

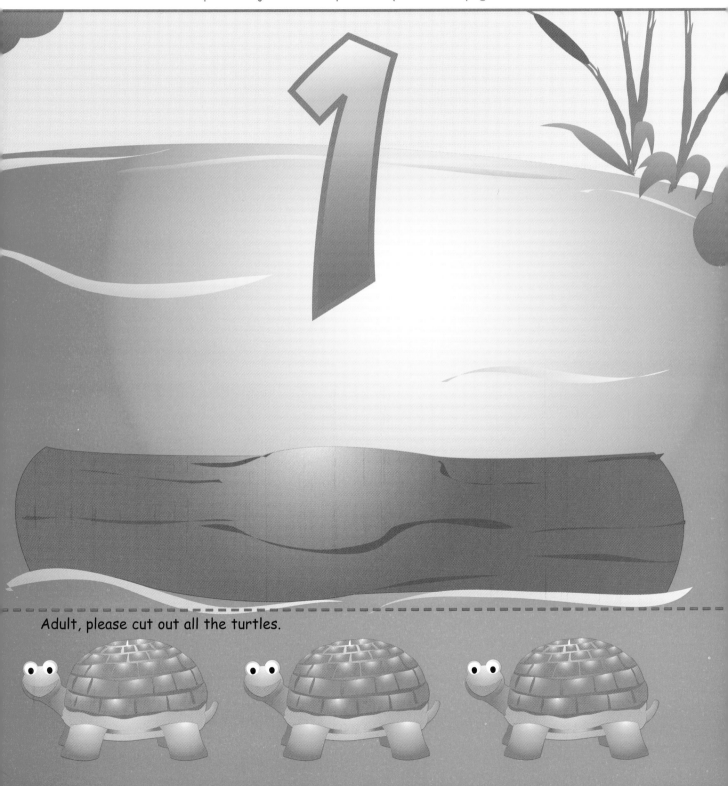

ACTIVITY 24

One Turtle

Directions: On the next twelve pages, your child will learn numbers 1–10 while practicing pasting objects to a specific spot on the page. Cut the three turtles from the bottom of the page. Count them with your child, touching each one as you count. Tell your child to paste one turtle on the log. Use the extra pieces in a fun extension activity on page 197.

Learn numbers 1–10 and place objects on a specific spot on the page.

Adult, please cut out all the turtles.

Two Frogs

Directions: Your child will learn numbers while practicing pasting objects to a specific spot on the page. Cut all three frogs from the bottom of the page. Count them with your child, touching each one as you count. Then, tell your child to paste two frogs on the lily pad. Use the extra piece in a fun extension activity on page 197.

Learn numbers 1–10 and place objects on a specific spot on the page.

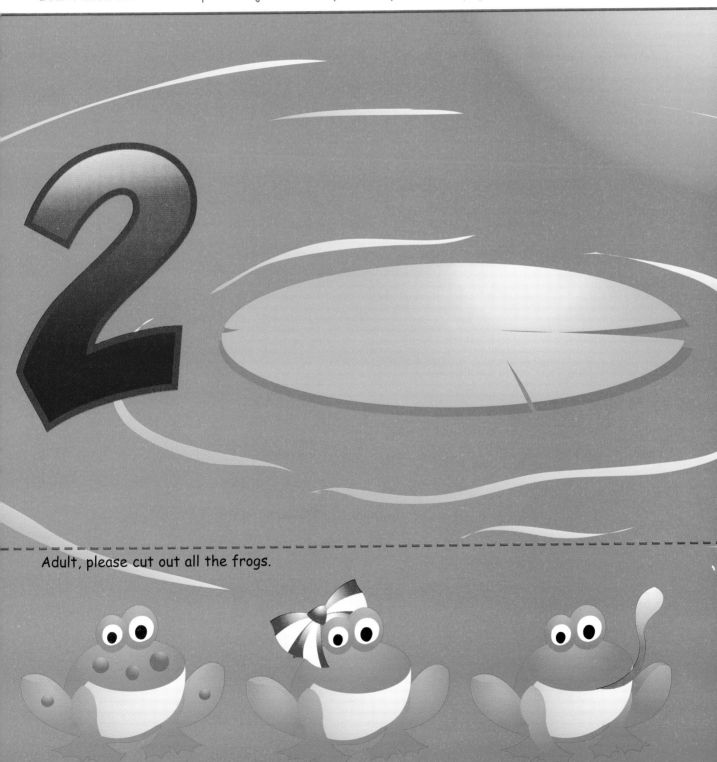

Adult, please cut out all the frogs.

ACTIVITY 26

Three Balls

Directions: Your child will learn numbers while practicing pasting objects to a specific spot on the page. Cut all five balls from the bottom of the page. Count them with your child, touching each one as you count. Then, tell your child to paste three balls in the air above the clown's head. Use the extra pieces in a fun extension activity on page 197.

Learn numbers 1–10 and place objects on a specific spot on the page.

Adult, please cut out all the balls.

ACTIVITY 27

Review Numbers 1-3

Directions: Your child will learn numbers while practicing pasting objects to a specific spot on the page. Cut all six pieces from the bottom of the page. Count them with your child, touching each piece as you count. Then, tell your child to paste them on the buildings below. Your child will paste one piece on Building 1, two pieces on Building 2, and 3 pieces on Building 3. Ask your child which building is the tallest and which is the shortest. Look for a fun extension activity on page 197.

Learn numbers 1-10 and place objects on a specific spot on the page.

Building 1   Building 2   Building 3

Adult, please cut out all the pieces.

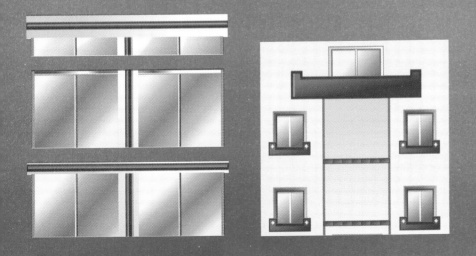

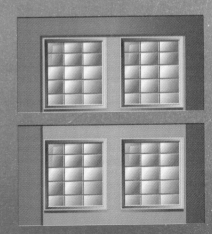

Four Windows

Directions: Your child will learn numbers while practicing pasting objects to a specific spot on the page. Cut all six windows from the bottom of the page. Count them with your child, touching each window as you count. Then, tell your child to paste four windows on the house. Use the extra pieces in a fun extension activity on page 197.

Learn numbers 1–10 and place objects on a specific spot on the page.

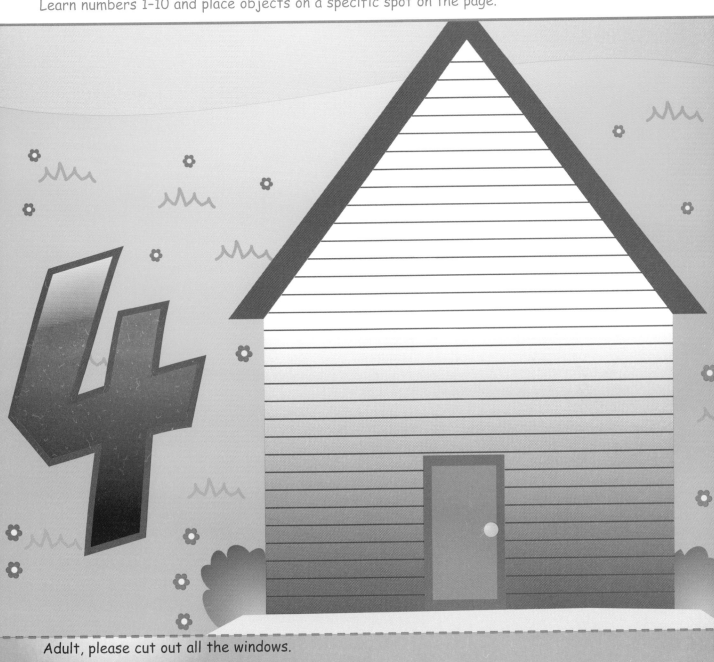

Adult, please cut out all the windows.

ACTIVITY 29

Flower Petals

Directions: Your child will learn numbers while practicing pasting objects to a specific spot on the page. Cut all seven petals from the bottom of the page. See if your child can count them on his or her own. Tell your child to paste five petals on the flower. Use the extra pieces in a fun extension activity on page 197.

Learn numbers 1–10 and place objects on a specific spot on the page.

Adult, please cut out all the petals.

Watercolor Paint

Directions: Your child will learn numbers while practicing pasting objects to a specific spot on the page. Cut all eight paint cakes from the bottom of the page. See if your child can count them on his or her own. Then, tell your child to paste six of his or her favorite colors onto the paint set. This is great opportunity to review colors!

Learn numbers 1–10 and place objects on a specific spot on the page.

Adult, please cut out all the paint cakes.

ACTIVITY 31

Review Numbers 4–6

Directions: Your child will learn numbers while practicing pasting objects to a specific spot on the page. Cut all six circles from the bottom of the page. Tell your child to count the number of circles already in the graph and paste the extra circles to finish the graph. Your child will paste two more circles in column "4," one more circle in column "5," and three more circles in column "6." Look for a fun extension activity on page 197.

Learn numbers 1–10 and place objects on a specific spot on the page.

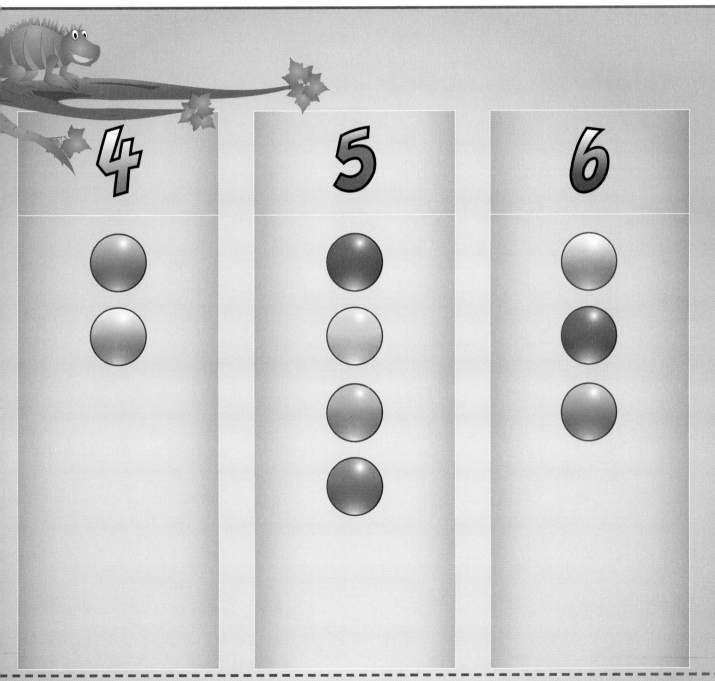

Adult, please cut out all the circles.

ACTIVITY 32

Gumball Machine

Directions: Your child will learn numbers while practicing pasting objects to a specific spot on the page. Cut all nine gumballs from the bottom of the page. See if your child can count them on his or her own. Then, tell your child to paste seven gumballs in the gumball machine. Use the extra pieces in a fun extension activity on page 197.

Learn numbers 1–10 and place objects on a specific spot on the page.

Adult, please cut out all the gumballs.

ACTIVITY 33

Spider's Legs

Directions: Your child will learn numbers while practicing pasting objects to a specific spot on the page. Cut all ten spider legs from the bottom of the page. See if your child is able to count to ten. Offer lots of encouragement and praise for his or her effort! Then, tell your child to paste eight spider legs on the spider's body, four legs on each side. Use the extra pieces in a fun extension activity on page 197.

Learn numbers 1–10 and place objects on a specific spot on the page.

Adult, please cut out all the spider legs.

Cozy Quilt

Directions: Your child will learn numbers while practicing pasting objects to a specific spot on the page. Cut all eleven quilt patches from the bottom of the page. See if your child can count them on his or her own. Then, tell your child to paste nine quilt patches to finish the cozy quilt. Ask your child how many quilt patches he or she has left. Your child just learned the basics of subtraction! Use the extra pieces in a fun extension activity on page 197.

Learn numbers 1–10 and place objects on a specific spot on the page.

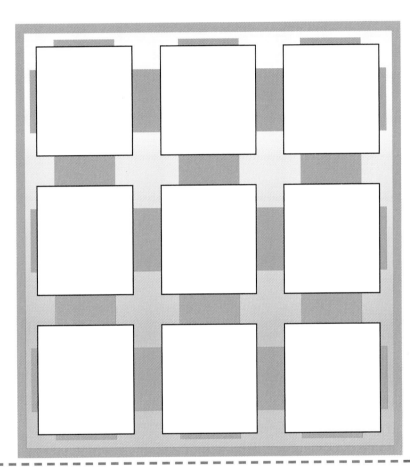

Adult, please cut out all the quilt patches.

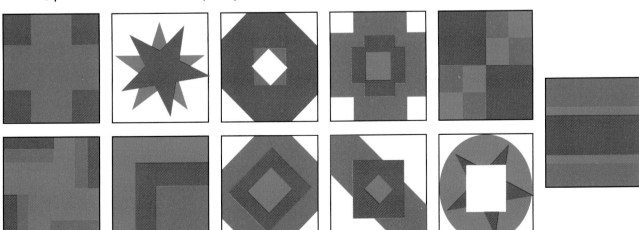

Watermelon

Directions: Your child will learn numbers while practicing pasting objects to a specific spot on the page. Cut all twelve watermelon seeds from the bottom of the page. See if your child can count to twelve without your help. Then, tell your child to paste ten watermelon seeds onto the juicy watermelon. Practice subtraction again and ask your child how many seeds he or she has left. Use the extra pieces in a fun extension activity on page 197.

Learn numbers 1–10 and place objects on a specific spot on the page.

Adult, please cut out all the watermelon seeds.

ACTIVITY 36

Funny Flamingo

Directions: Your child will practice pasting pieces together to finish a puzzle. Cut out the puzzle pieces for your child. He or she will arrange the pieces of the puzzle to make a picture and then paste them on the page.

Paste pieces together to finish a puzzle.

Adult, please cut out the pieces.

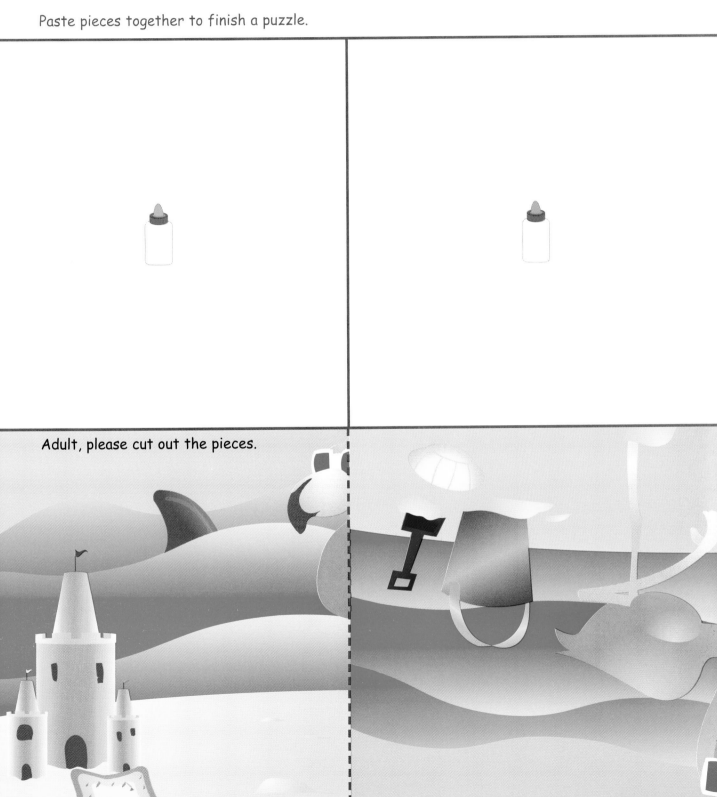

ACTIVITY 37

Dog Ears

Directions: Now, your child will practice following directions and placing objects on a page to complete a picture. Cut the ears from the bottom of the page and then show your child how to place them on the page so that they cover the designated spaces. Say: *Paste the spotted ear on the dog first, then paste the brown ear.* It is okay if your child does not match up the ears exactly. His or her skills will develop over time!

Follow the directions to complete the picture.

Adult, please cut out the ears.

 ACTIVITY 38 — Ice Cream Treat

Directions: Your child will practice following directions and placing objects on a page to complete a picture. Cut the ice cream scoops from the side of the page. Then, have your child follow your directions to complete the picture. Say: *Paste the strawberry scoop on top of the vanilla scoop*, or, *Paste the vanilla scoop on first and the strawberry scoop on next.*

Follow the directions to complete the picture.

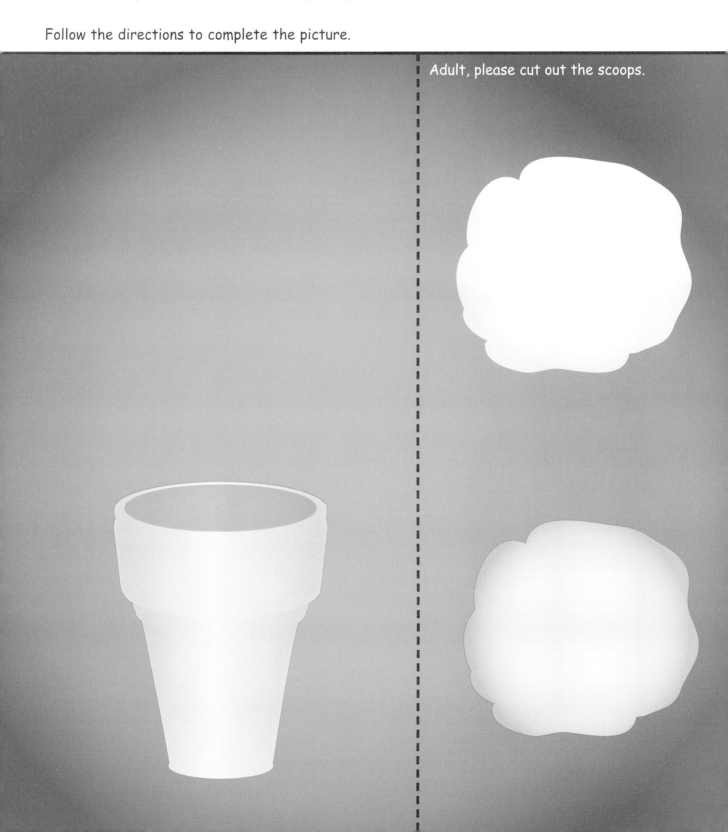

Adult, please cut out the scoops.

Build a Snowman

Directions: Your child will practice following directions and placing objects on a page to complete a picture. Cut the snowman parts from the bottom of the page. Have your child follow your directions. Say: *First, paste the biggest snowball on the bottom. Next, paste the big snowball on top of the biggest snowball. Last, paste the small snowball on the top.* It's important for your child to be familiar with direction words like *first*, *next*, and *last*.

Follow the directions to complete the picture.

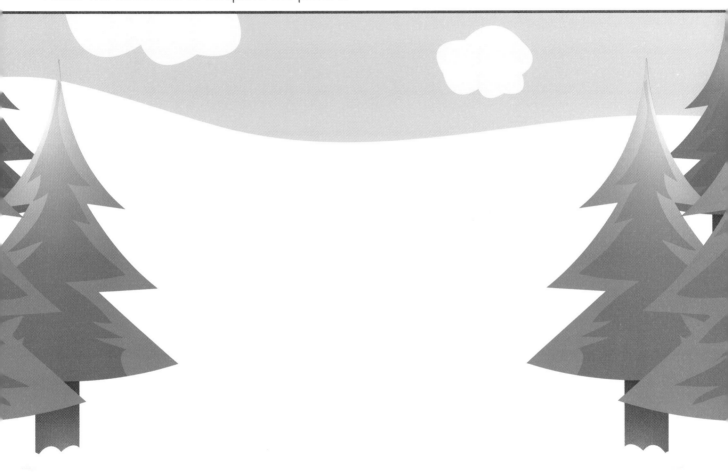

Adult, please cut out the snowman pieces.

ACTIVITY 41

Dinner Time!

Directions: Your child will practice following directions and placing objects on a page to complete a picture. He or she will also review numbers in this activity. Cut the food out from the bottom of the page. Say: *First, paste the pork chop over the number one. Next, paste the peaches over the number two. Last, paste the salad over the number three.* Take this opportunity to discuss healthy eating habits with your child!

Follow the directions to complete the picture.

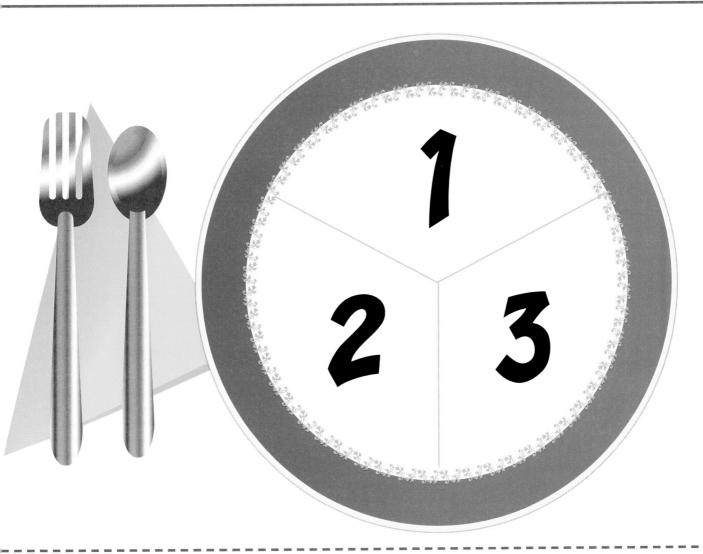

Adult, please cut out the food.

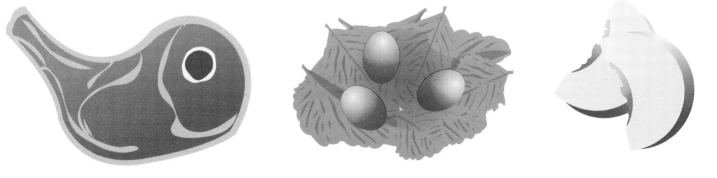

ACTIVITY 42

Ice Cream Truck Puzzle

Directions: Your child will practice pasting pieces together to finish a puzzle. Cut out the puzzle pieces for your child. He or she will arrange the pieces of the puzzle to make a picture and then paste them on the page.

Paste pieces together to finish a puzzle.

Adult, please cut out the pieces.

Turtle Shell

Directions: Here, your child will practice pasting a cut-out to the corresponding blank space in the picture. Cut the oval from the bottom of the page. Your child will paste the cut-out on the turtle so that it covers the white space. This activity requires a lot of fine motor control. Encourage your child to keep trying, and resist the urge to do it yourself! Don't worry if your child does not match up the oval exactly. Show him or her how to use the markings on the turtle to guide the placement of the oval.

Paste a cut-out to fill a blank space in the picture.

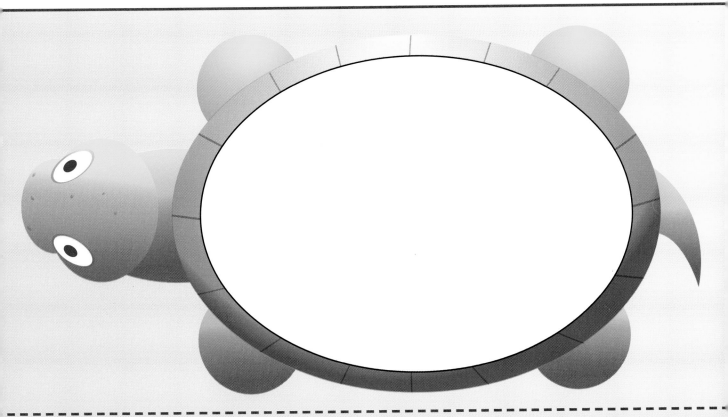

Adult, please cut out the oval.

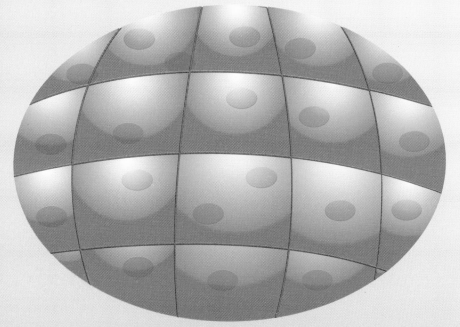

 **ACTIVITY 44**

Baseball

Directions: Your child will practice pasting a cut-out to the corresponding blank space in the picture. Cut the square from the bottom of the page. Your child will paste it onto the baseball so that it covers the white space. Don't worry if your child does not match up the square exactly. Show him or her how to use the red stitching to guide the placement of the square.

Paste a cut-out to fill a blank space in the picture.

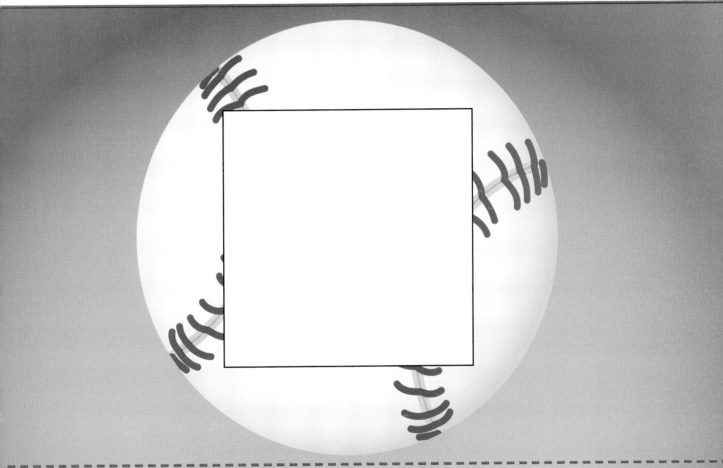

Adult, please cut out the square.

 # Circles

Directions: In this section, your child will learn shapes while reviewing basic pasting skills. Cut the circles from the bottom of the page. Show them to your child and ask him or her to identify the shape. Then, have your child glue the circles on the page to finish the picture.

Learn shapes while reviewing basic pasting skills.

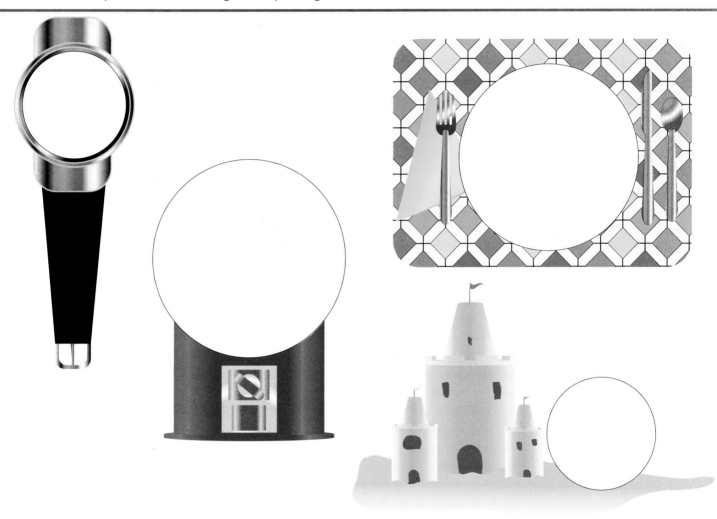

Adult, please cut out the circles.

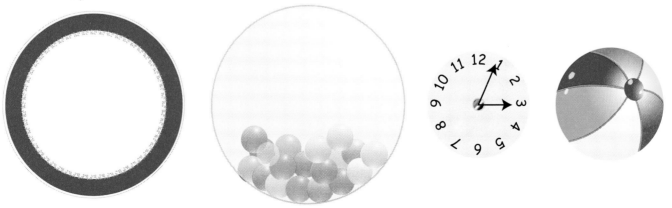

ACTIVITY 46

Squares

Directions: Your child will learn shapes while reviewing basic pasting skills. Cut the squares from the bottom of the page. Show them to your child and ask him or her to identify the shape. Then, have your child glue the squares on the page to finish the picture.

Learn shapes while reviewing basic pasting skills.

Adult, please cut out the squares.

ACTIVITY 48

Triangles

Directions: Your child will learn shapes while reviewing basic pasting skills. Cut the triangles from the bottom of the page. Show them to your child and ask him or her to identify the shape. Then, have your child glue the triangles on the page to finish the picture. You can use this activity to introduce patterns to your child. Can he or she see a pattern in the triangles on the snake's back? Can he or she complete the pattern by pasting the triangles in the right places?

Learn shapes while reviewing basic pasting skills.

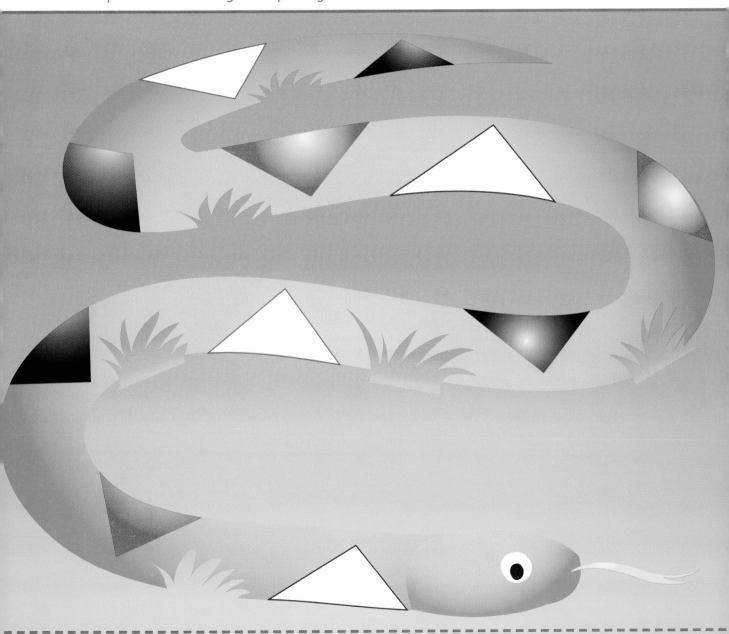

Adult, please cut out the triangles.

Hearts

Directions: Your child will learn shapes while reviewing basic pasting skills. Cut the heart halves from the bottom of the page. Show your child how to put them together with the heart pieces on the page to complete the hearts. Then, have your child glue the heart halves on the page to finish the picture.

Learn shapes while reviewing basic pasting skills.

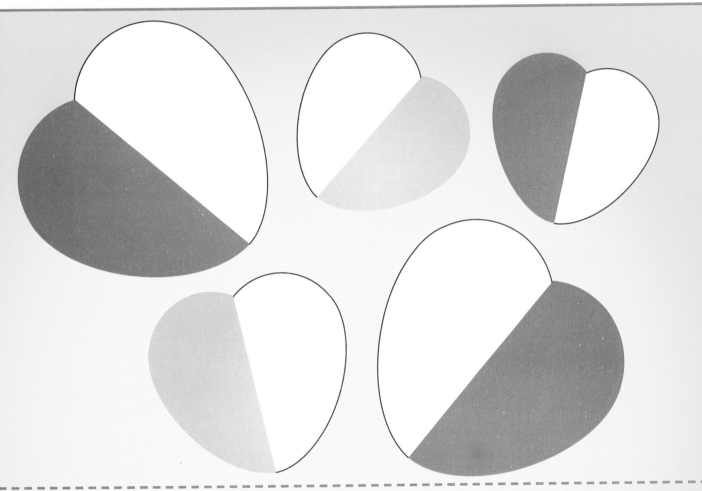

Adult, please cut out the heart pieces.

ACTIVITY 50

Alphabet Book

Directions: In this section, your child will use his or her pasting skills to create an alphabet book. Remove pages 121, 123, 125, and 139. Cut out the rectangles that contain the lowercase letters and their corresponding pictures. Your child will paste the lowercase letters onto the matching uppercase letter pages. Once your child has completed all the alphabet pages, remove the pages from the book and separate the top halves from the bottom halves by cutting along the dotted lines. To help your child assemble the book, punch holes on the left side of each page and use yarn or brass brads to bind the book together. Now, your child has his or her very own alphabet book!

Encourage your child to add to this book by placing corresponding stickers, photographs, and magazine pictures on the back of each letter page. He or she can practice learning the letters of the alphabet by tracing the letters on each page with his or her finger.

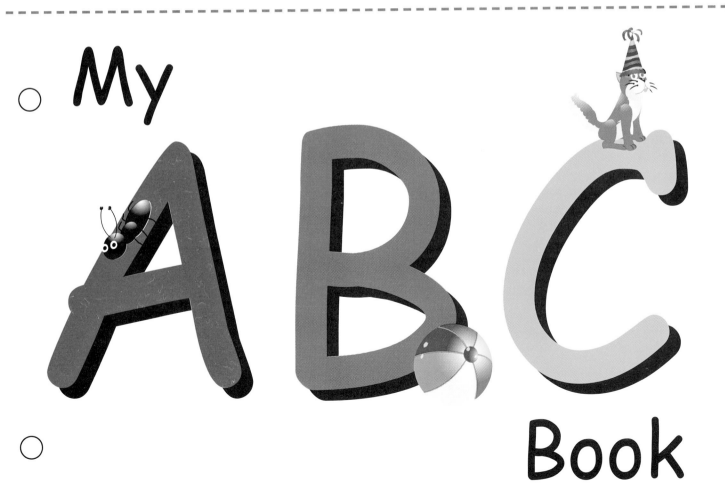

My ABC Book

ACTIVITY 52

Who's in the Zoo?

Directions: Your child will practice matching and pasting odd shapes to finish a picture. He or she will use the skills learned thus far to complete this activity. Cut out the pieces for your child. Your child will arrange the pieces on the page. Then, he or she will paste them on to finish the picture. Can your child tell you who is in the zoo?

Match and paste odd shapes to finish a picture.

Adult, please cut out the pieces.

Hot Air Balloon

Directions: Your child will practice matching and pasting odd shapes to finish a picture. He or she will use the skills learned thus far to complete this activity. Cut out the pieces for your child. Your child will arrange the pieces on the page. Then, he or she will paste them on to finish the picture.

Match and paste odd shapes to finish a picture.

Adult, please cut out the pieces.

Rubber Ducky Puzzle

Directions: Your child will practice pasting pieces together to finish a puzzle. Cut out the puzzle pieces for your child. He or she will arrange the pieces of the puzzle to make a picture and then paste them on the page.

Paste pieces together to finish a puzzle.

Adult, please cut out the pieces.

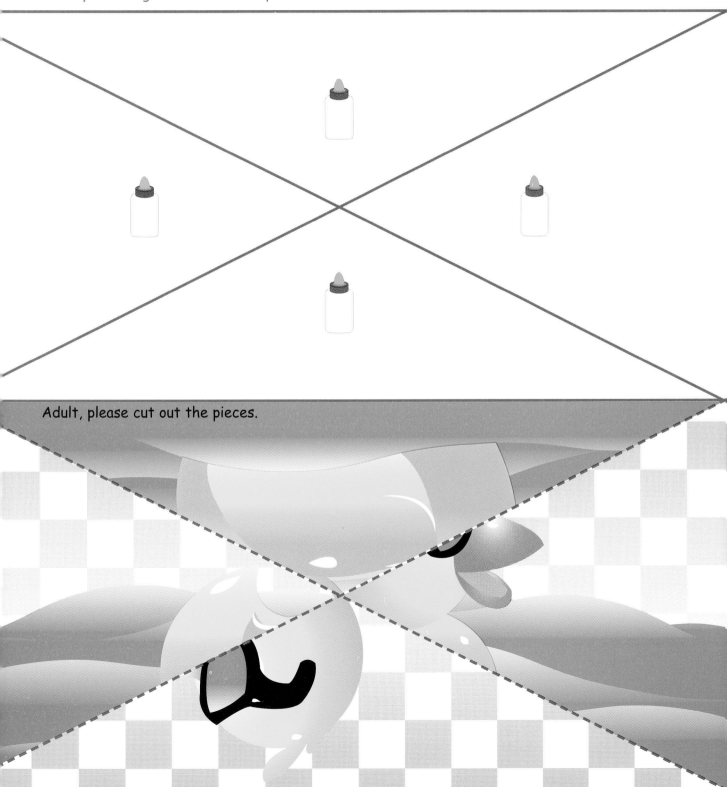

Sea of Fish: Pattern Block Triangles

Directions: This section introduces a math manipulative called *pattern blocks*. Your child will use pattern blocks often in school. They help teach geometry, symmetry, fractions, and other early math skills. Your child will practice pasting pattern blocks on a page to make a picture. Cut out the shapes below and tell your child to paste the *triangles* on the page to finish the fish tails. Save the extra shapes from each activity. Your child can use them to practice building pictures!

Paste pattern block shapes on a page to make a picture.

Adult, please cut out the shapes.

ACTIVITY 56

Boats: Pattern Block Trapezoids

Directions: In this activity, your child will practice pasting pattern block shapes on a page to make a picture. Cut out the shapes below and tell your child to paste the *trapezoids* on the page to finish the boats.

Paste pattern block shapes on a page to make a picture.

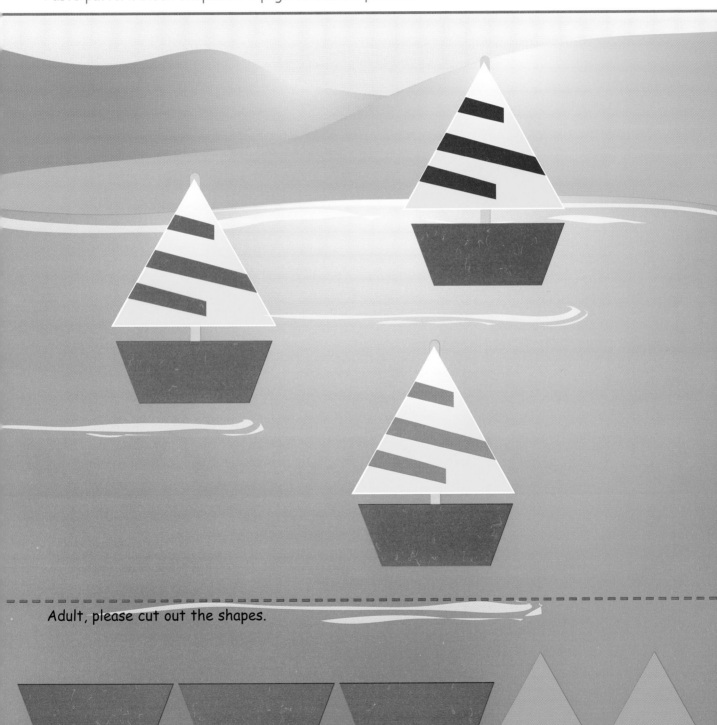

Adult, please cut out the shapes.

Garden: Pattern Block Hexagons

Directions: In this activity, your child will practice pasting pattern block shapes on a page to make a picture. Cut out the shapes below. Point out the hexagons to your child. How many sides does a hexagon have? On a separate piece of paper, trace around one of the hexagons. Number the sides as your child counts them. Then, tell your child to paste the *hexagons* to the page to finish the flowers.

Paste pattern block shapes on a page to make a picture.

Adult, please cut out the shapes.

Taxicab Puzzle

Directions: Your child will practice pasting pieces together to finish a puzzle. Cut out the puzzle pieces for your child. He or she will arrange the pieces of the puzzle to make a picture and then paste them on the page.

Paste pieces together to finish a puzzle.

Adult, please cut out the pieces.

Kites: Pattern Block Parallelograms

Directions: In this activity, your child will practice pasting pattern block shapes on a page to make a picture. Cut out the shapes below. Then, tell your child to paste the *parallelograms* to the page to finish the kites. Ask your child if he or she knows another name for this shape. (It's also called a *diamond*.)

Paste pattern block shapes on a page to make a picture.

Adult, please cut out the shapes.

ACTIVITY 60

Houses: Pattern Block Squares

Directions: In this activity, your child will practice pasting pattern block shapes on a page to make a picture. Cut out the shapes below. Then, tell your child to paste the *squares* on the page to finish the houses.

Paste pattern block shapes on a page to make a picture.

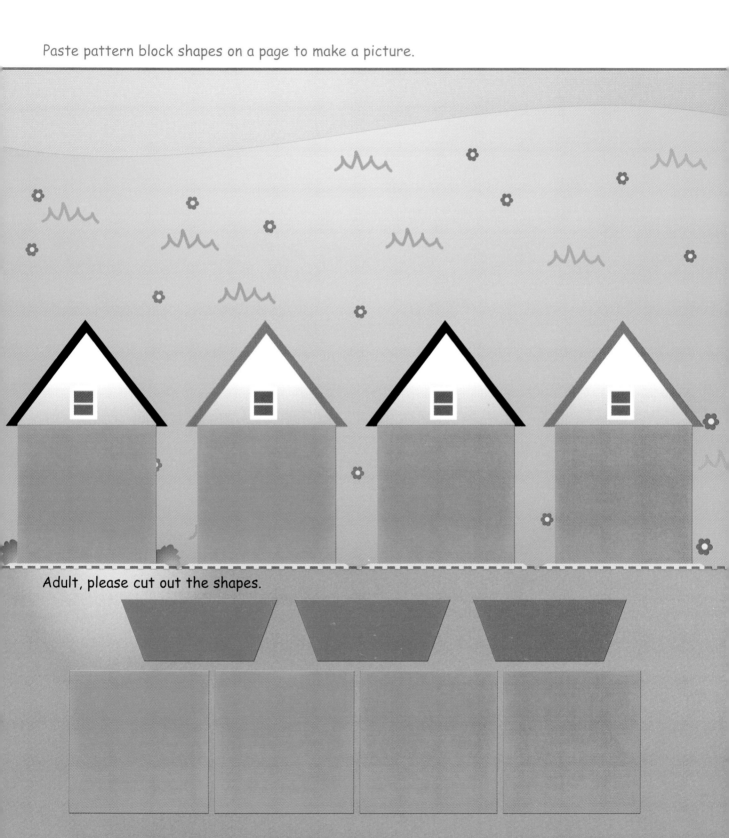

Adult, please cut out the shapes.

Masterpiece!

Directions: Now, your child will practice using pattern blocks to build his or her own masterpiece. Cut out the pattern block shapes below and combine them with the leftover shapes from the previous activities. Explore them with your child as he or she uses them to make different designs. Ask your child if he or she can name some of the shapes. At the end of the exploration time, instruct your child to paste the shapes in the open space below in any design he or she chooses.

Paste pattern block shapes on a page to make a picture.

Adult, please cut out the shapes.

ACTIVITY 62

Rub-A-Dub-Dub Puzzle

Directions: Your child will practice pasting pieces together to finish a puzzle. Cut out the puzzle pieces for your child. Your child will arrange the pieces of the puzzle to find out who is taking a long, bubbly bath.

Paste pieces together to finish a puzzle.

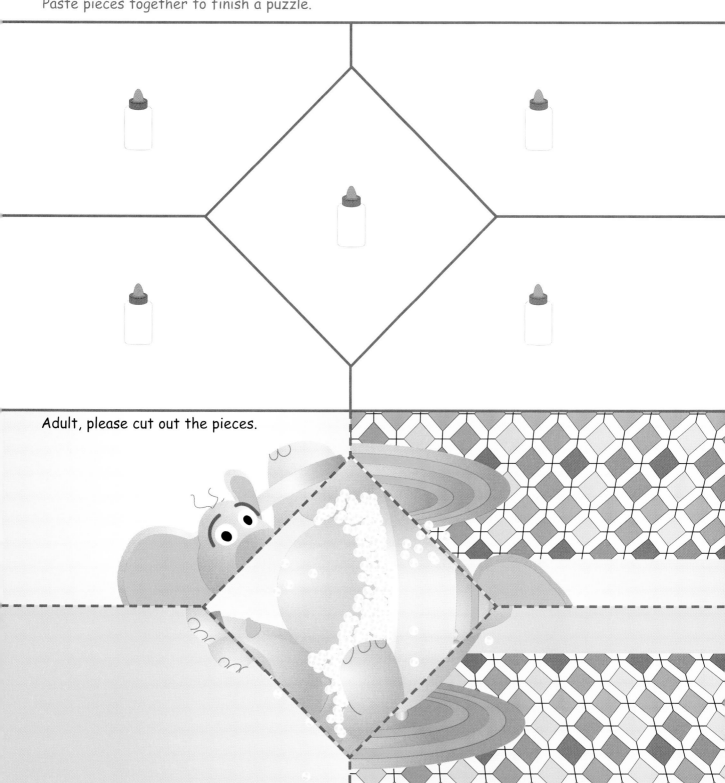

Adult, please cut out the pieces.

Big Skills for Little Hands is an exciting new series that provides hands-on activities to develop hand-eye coordination, fine motor skills, early writing skills, and print awareness in young children. The other books in this series are similar to *I Can Paste!* and include extension activities, helpful hints for fine motor development, and write-and-wipe activities for the board in the back of the book.

The *Big Skills for Little Hands* series also includes these titles:

The following pages feature sample activities from the other titles in the *Big Skills for Little Hands* series. The activities in this series are designed for you and your child to complete together. Your child will have fun and learn new skills while spending quality time with you!

In this series, the pages ARE the activities! Toddlers and preschoolers will manipulate the paper in the books by cutting it, pasting on it, drawing on it, coloring it, folding it, and tracing it. All the pages are perforated to make each activity easier to complete and to make displaying finished work a snap.

I Can Cut!, teaches your child the basics of using scissors. Your child will develop his or her fine motor skills while learning to cut straight lines, curvy lines, shapes, and more!

In *I Can Fold!*, your child will manipulate paper to make cards and play items and learn some basic origami techniques.

I Can Color!, *I Can Trace!*, and *I Can Draw!* will give your child an opportunity to develop the correct writing utensil grip and enhance his or her visual discrimination. The drawing, tracing, and coloring activities will help develop your child's confidence in writing, color recognition, and direction-following skills.

Remember, you are your child's first teacher. The time you spend together is an important part of his or her development. The books in this series will help guide you through activities that are beneficial to your child during this crucial time of development. Have fun working through these books together and watching your child bloom and grow!

Hidden Tiger

Directions: Your child will practice cutting a straight line. Your child should now be able to cut along the dotted lines without your help. First, your child should cut the top half of the picture from the bottom half. Then, your child should cut the along the dotted lines on the bottom half to make blades of grass. Your child can put the tiger behind the grass and let him peek out from behind. Your child can also help the tiger practice his hunting skills by making him jump out from behind the grass!

Cut a straight line.

Racetrack Racers

Directions: Your child will practice cutting a curved line. Your child will cut out the racetrack. You can help by cutting out the racecars for the track and folding them down the middle. Then, you and your child can race to the finish line! This is a good opportunity to introduce position words like *first* and *last*.

Cut a curved line.

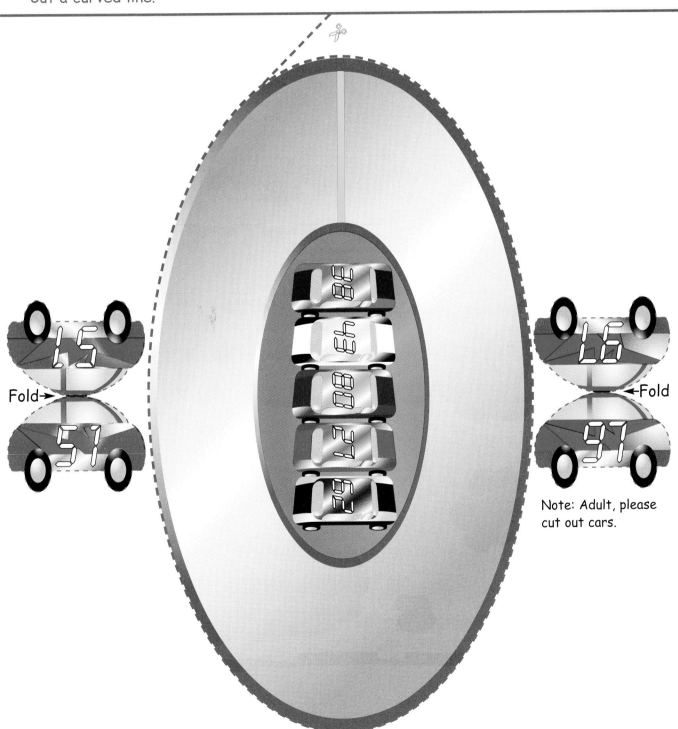

Fold→

←Fold

Note: Adult, please cut out cars.

Delicious Cookies

Directions: Your child will practice cutting a square and a circle. Your child will cut along the dotted lines in this picture to make a wonderful assortment of cookies! Have a cookie party with your child. Use the pizza pan from page 101 as a serving plate. Your child can practice basic math skills by sorting, counting, and distributing the cookies equally among all the party guests.

Cut a square and circle.

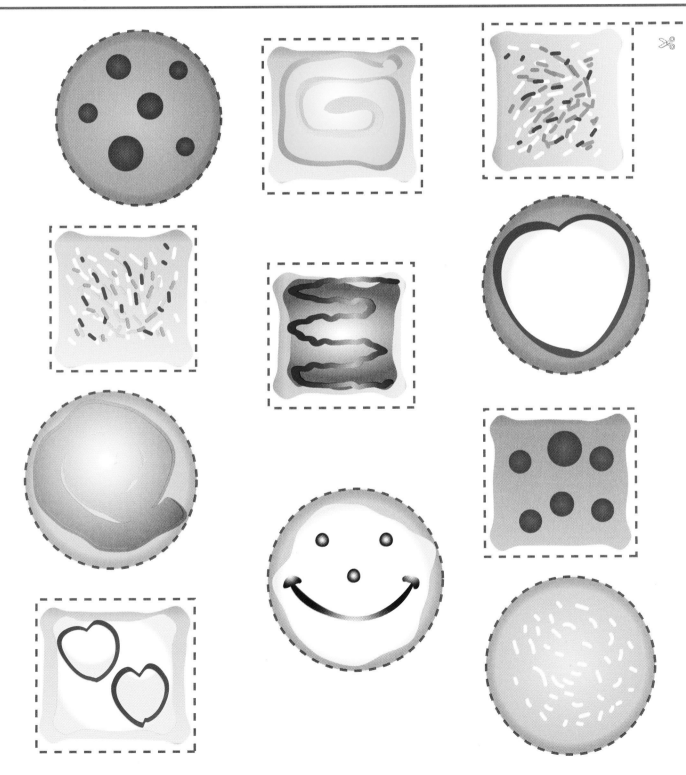

ACTIVITY 66

"Happy Birthday!" Card

Directions: In the following activities, your child will practice folding paper in half. Folding paper helps build manual dexterity and mental focus. In this activity, your child will fold the paper in half along the blue line to make a birthday card for someone special. Help your child write a special message on the inside. Then, let your child sign his or her name on the card.

Fold paper in half.

ACTIVITY
67

Camping Tent

Directions: Your child will practice folding paper in half. He or she will fold the paper in half to make a camping tent. You can help by cutting out the campers, the tent, and the campfire. Show your child how to fold the campers and campfire in half so that they will stand up. Then, pretend you and your child are on a camping trip. Take turns telling silly stories by the campfire!

Fold paper in half.

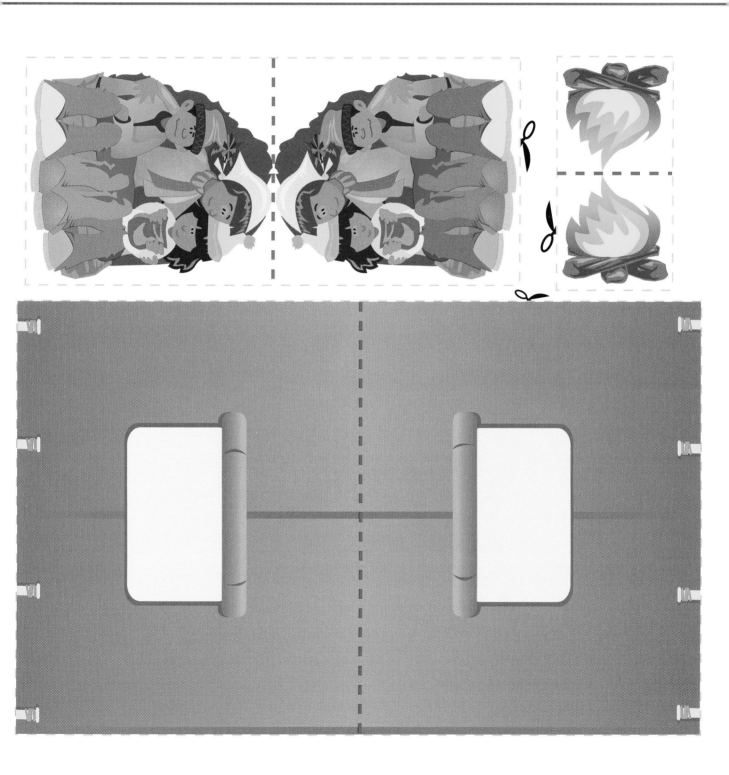

Beautiful Bird

Directions: Your child will practice folding paper to create an accordion fold. Cut out the wing pieces below. Your child will follow the blue and green lines to fold the wing pieces like an accordion. Help your child finish the bird by cutting out the bird's body and stapling the wings to either side of the bird's body. Punch a hole at the top of the bird. Your child can thread string through the hole to make a beautiful bird mobile.

Use an accordion fold.

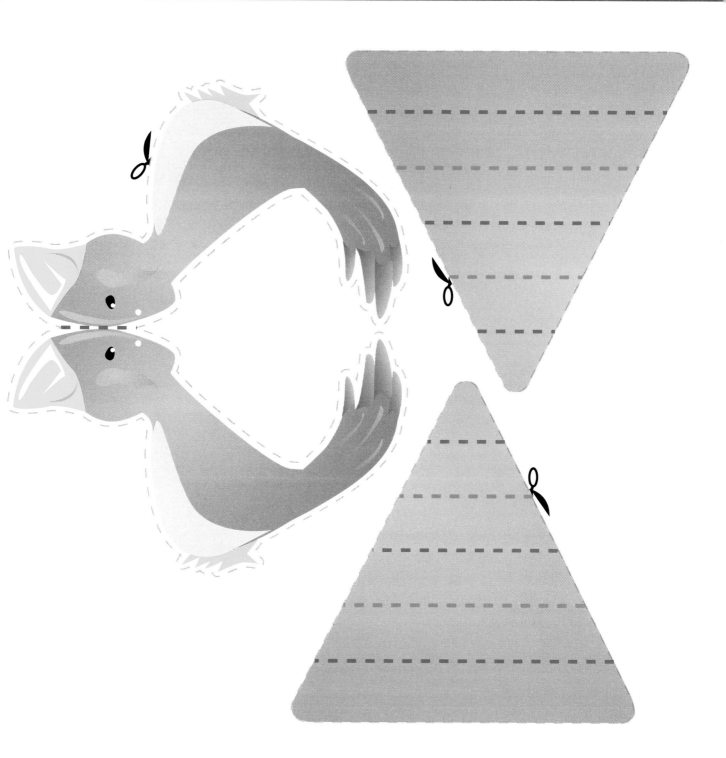

Crayons

Directions: Your child will color a blank area to complete the picture. Your child will use three colors to color the crayons. This activity is a great time to review color names. Tell your child your favorite color and ask him or her to tell you the color he or she likes best!

Color the blank areas to complete the picture.

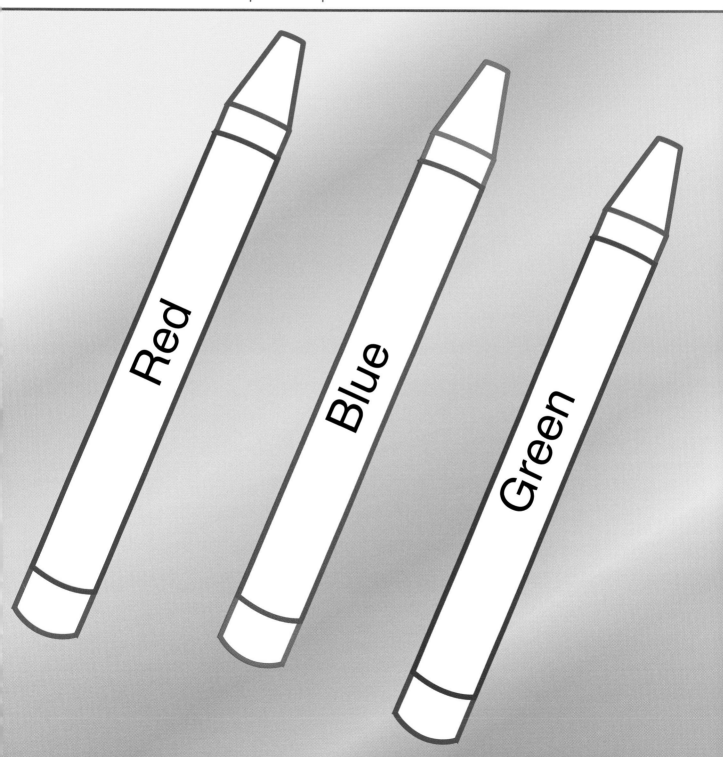

ACTIVITY 70

Pick Your Flavor

Directions: Your child will color a blank area to complete the picture. Your child will color the ice cream scoop to make his or her favorite flavor. Yum! You can help by writing the flavor on the line next to the picture. Touch the word and say the name of the flavor.

Color the blank area to complete the picture.

My favorite flavor is

_____.

71 Yellow Star

Directions: Now, your child will practice using the correct color to fill in the blank space in the picture. On this page, your child will finish coloring the yellow star. As your child is coloring, ask him or her to think of other things that are yellow.

Use the correct color to fill in the blank space.

ACTIVITY 72

Hungry Bunny

Directions: Now, your child will practice tracing a path. Help your child trace the bunny tracks to help the bunny get to the carrot. See if he or she can complete the activity without doing the warm-up exercise. Show your child how to follow the path by moving from one set of bunny tracks to another.

Trace a path.

ACTIVITY 73

Kite Confusion

Directions: Your child will practice tracing a path. By tracing the lines from the animals to the kites, your child will help the dog and cat determine to whom each kite belongs. Because your child will be tracing multiple lines, tracing the lines with his or her finger before completing the activity will be very helpful.

Trace a path.

Guess the Surprise

Directions: Your child will practice tracing an odd shape. Your child should trace the shape, starting at the dot, with his or her finger before using a pencil to complete the activity. Ask your child if he or she can guess what is under the wrapping paper. (Hint: It has two wheels and pedals!)

Trace an odd shape.

ACTIVITY 75

Numbers: Seven Dots

Directions: Your child will practice following directions to draw the correct number of objects. There is one dot on the ladybug. Your child will draw six more dots to make a total of seven dots. Then, you should point to the dots and count out loud with your child.

Draw six more dots.

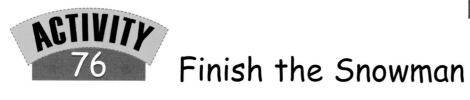

ACTIVITY 76
Finish the Snowman

Directions: Your child will practice completing a picture without using tracing lines. Your child will finish drawing the picture of the snowman. Then, he or she can draw snowballs on the ground next to the snowman.

Complete the other half of the picture.

ACTIVITY 77

Draw a Spider

Directions: Your child will practice following directions to draw a picture. Your child will follow the directions below to draw a picture of a spider. You can lightly trace the shapes to give your child a guide to follow, but give your child a chance to do it independently first.

Follow directions to draw a picture.

1. Draw 1 ● in the center of the page to make a body.
2. Draw 1 ● on top of the big circle to make a head.
3. Draw 8 ∧ around the big circle to make legs.
4. Draw 2 • in the small circle to make eyes.

Fine Motor Activities to do Around the House

Try these fun pasting activities at home! As your child is working, try not to correct his or her work or add too much input. Keep in mind that the process, not the finished product, is what is important!

Extensions for pasting activities

For use after Activity #1 on pages 15–17:
Help your child make a collage book! Paste or draw a large letter in the middle of the paper. Your child will find pictures that begin with that letter sound and paste them around the letter. Focus first on letters that are in your child's name. Then, branch out to other letters in the alphabet.

For use after Activity #2 on pages 19–21
Your child can use the chain he or she created in Activity #2 or paste together strips of scrap paper to create a chain. Your child can use the chain as a calendar counting down to special events. He or she will tear off one link each day. This is a great subtraction activity!

Your child can also make a Memory Chain. Help your child by writing a milestone or a memory of a special day on a paper link. Your child will keep adding paper links to create a chain of memories!

For use after Activities #24–35 on pages 67–91:
Provide your child with lots of interesting pictures from magazines. You can also let your child tear small pieces of scrap paper or use the extra pictures from the counting pages. Give your child a blank sheet of paper and some glue. He or she will glue the pictures and scraps onto the paper to create a collage. Observe the photos and pictures that he or she selects for the collage. As your child works, talk about the pictures that are on the collage. Why did he or she choose them? Encourage your child to cover the entire piece of paper with pictures.

For use after Activities #24–35 on pages 67–91:
Collect or buy craft sticks. Write numerals on one set of craft sticks. Add some tempera paint to white glue. Help your child place colored dots of glue on the other set of sticks to correspond with the numerals. Let the glue dry. Then you and your child can play a matching game, matching the numerals to the dots by counting the dried glue dots on the sticks. See if your child can close his or her eyes and count the number of raised dots on a stick by using his or her fingers.

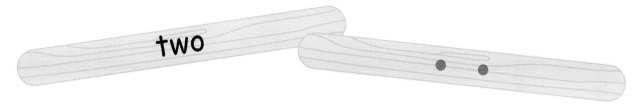

For use after the puzzle activities:
Choose pictures from magazines. Cut the picture into halves or fourths. Give them to your child to reassemble and glue onto a piece of paper.

More pasting activities

Glue Glop

Gather several small glue bottles. Add a teaspoon of tempera paint to each bottle, using a different color in each. Stir with a craft stick. Open the tips of the bottles so that only a small amount of glue can come out.

Give your child a white piece of paper and let him or her drizzle glue on to the paper. Encourage your child to move the bottles around and look at the patterns he or she is creating. Not only is this tons of fun for little hands, but it is also a very soothing activity for children. Store your child's creation in a safe place, away from curious hands, and let it dry.

Dot-to-Dot

Mix glue with tempera paint. Help your child place dots of glue on a piece of paper. Let the glue dry. Then, your child can use a crayon to connect the dots.

Your child can also lay a piece of paper over the top of the dried glue and use the side of a crayon to create a rubbing of the dots. He or she can move the paper around and switch crayon colors to create a unique piece of art.

3-D Sculptures

Collect juice bottle caps, foam packing pieces, empty containers, uncooked pasta, dry cereal, cotton balls, cotton swabs, and any other items your child could use to create a sculpture. Your child will use glue to build a sculpture using the materials you provide. This activity provides a great opportunity to talk about ways to recycle or re-use items you might otherwise throw away!

Window Decoration

Provide your child with buttons, a margarine container lid, and a long piece of string. He or she will cover the inside of the lid with a thick layer of glue and add the buttons. You will place the hanging string in the glue so that a good portion of it is hanging off of the glued section and set the lid aside to dry. Then, pop the dried glue out of the lid and hang the decoration in your child's bedroom window. Now, your child has a beautiful window decoration!

Colored Rice Mosaic

Place a cup of long grain rice (not instant) into a zippered plastic bag along with a few drops of food coloring and one tablespoon of rubbing alcohol. Let your child shake the bag vigorously until all the rice is colored. Spread the rice on a sheet of waxed paper to dry. Use a new baggie for each color of rice you create. Thin some glue by pouring it into a small cup and adding water until the glue is thin enough to be "painted" easily. Have your child paint a patch of glue on a piece of heavyweight paper. Then, he or she will pinch the colored rice on the glued area. He or she will continue gluing and pinching until the entire paper is covered. This is a great activity for developing the small muscles in your child's hands!

Fine motor extension activities

Bean Sort
Sorting beans provides practice picking up small objects with the thumb and forefinger. Place a variety of dried beans into a large container. Have your child practice sorting the beans into the different sections of an empty ice cube tray.

Where's My Top?
Provide a large assortment of plastic bottles and their lids in a bin. Have your child sort through the lids and bottles to see if he or she can match all the tops to the bottoms.

Typing
Allow your child chances to type letters and numbers on a typewriter or computer keyboard. This not only enhances fine motor skills, but also letter and number recognition. See if your child can type all the letters in his or her name, or pull lettered blocks or tiles out of a box and type the letters. If your child is using a computer, make sure the font is large enough that he or she can print out his or her work and copy the letters in his or her own handwriting.

Sawdust Pennies
Add several pennies to a sand table or large bin filled with sawdust. Invite your child to sort through the sawdust to find the pennies hidden inside. Change the activity by placing other small objects in the sawdust.

Magnets
Magnets fascinate children. Provide your child with an assortment of magnets, items that are attracted to magnets, and items that are not attracted to magnets. Have your child test the items and sort all the objects into two piles.

Hide and Seek Surprises
Place a small toy or sticker in a small container with a lid. Place this container inside a larger container, and these containers in an even larger container. Be sure to use containers that have variety of lift-off or screw-off lids. Hide the container inside a closet. Give your child clues where to find the boxes and then let him or her twist, pull, and pry his or her way to the surprise.

Stringing Beads, Pasta, and Cereal
Threading string through beads builds fine motor abilities. Dip the end of a piece of yarn or string in glue and let it dry. This will make the string easier to thread through the beads, pasta, or cereal.

For more fine motor practice your child can:
- Practice buttoning with large buttons.
- Play with clay and play dough.
- Use tweezers to pick up small beads, seeds, or cotton balls.
- Use salad tongs to pick up small toys during clean up.
- Peel stickers off of their backing.
- Set the table (grasping silverware uses the pincher motion).
- Use crayons when coloring (they require more hand pressure to get the color on the paper).

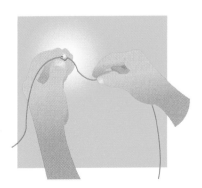

School Readiness Checklist

SCHOOL READINESS: Speech and Language Development

- ☐ Speaks in complete sentences.

- ☐ Speaks clearly enough to be understood by someone who does not know him or her well.

- ☐ Communicates well with peers.

- ☐ Can rhyme and recognizes rhyming sounds.

- ☐ Identifies the beginning sounds of some words.

- ☐ Identifies some alphabet letters.

- ☐ Tells the meaning of some simple words, like "stop."

- ☐ Can recite ABC's and count to ten.

- ☐ Asks questions.

- ☐ Looks at pictures and can tell stories about them.

- ☐ Can answer questions about a short story.

- ☐ Repeats phrases said by an adult.

- ☐ Can communicate with both adults and peers.

School Readiness Checklist

SCHOOL READINESS: Social Development

- ☐ Can be taken away from parents without being overly upset.

- ☐ Can spend extended periods of time away from parents.

- ☐ Explores and tries new things.

- ☐ Is curious and motivated to learn.

- ☐ Puts away toys and helps with family chores.

- ☐ Meets visitors without shyness.

- ☐ Able to stay on task and work independently.

- ☐ Finishes tasks.

- ☐ Describes some basic emotions and feelings.

- ☐ Expresses feelings and needs.

- ☐ Recognizes authority.

- ☐ Gets along and plays cooperatively with other children.

- ☐ Can take care of own toilet needs independently.

- ☐ Feels good about self and talks easily.

- ☐ Dresses self and cares for own belongings.

School Readiness Checklist

☐ Waits his or her turn.

☐ Exhibits self-control.

☐ Seeks out interactive play with other children.

☐ Listens to stories without interrupting.

☐ Uses words rather than physical aggression to get what he or she wants.

☐ Understands that actions have both causes and effects.

☐ Is beginning to share with others.

☐ Follows simple directions.

☐ Shows beginning of "empathy" skills.

☐ Knows parent's names, home address, and phone number.

☐ Can recite own first and last name.

☐ Says "please" and "thank you."

☐ Understands basic safety rules.
     Examples: Don't talk or get in a car with a stranger. Look both ways before crossing the street.

☐ Is aware of any food allergies he or she has.

☐ Can tell a story about a past event.

School Readiness Checklist

SCHOOL READINESS: Motor Skill Development

☐ Runs, jumps, skips, hops, and gallops.

☐ Can bounce and catch a ball.

☐ Walks backward.

☐ Walks up and down stairs alternating feet.

☐ Can walk in a straight line.

☐ Uses hand-eye coordination.
Examples: Can jump on one foot, stand on one foot for 5–10 seconds, clap hands.

☐ Holds a pencil or crayon correctly.

☐ Holds scissors and cuts correctly.

☐ Can use scissors and glue to cut and paste.

☐ Can trace basic shapes.

☐ Builds with construction toys and blocks.

☐ Draws and colors beyond simple scribbles.

☐ Can put a 10 to 12 piece puzzle together.

☐ Can button, zip up zippers, or snap clothing.

☐ Ties own shoes.

School Readiness Checklist

SCHOOL READINESS: Academic and General Knowledge

☐ Can write full name and recite address.

☐ Recognizes own first name in writing.

☐ Knows basic shapes.

☐ Knows colors.

☐ Knows relative sizes.
  Example: *big-small* or *small-smaller-smallest*

☐ Recognizes and completes patterns.

☐ Knows body parts, such as nose, ear, elbow.

☐ Can match similar objects and explain why they are alike.

☐ Can count to twenty.

☐ Knows ABC's and can recognize and write most letters.

☐ Can memorize things that have been read to him repeatedly.
  Example: Pretends to read a favorite story.

☐ Understands that print carries a message.

☐ Uses left to right progression.

School Readiness Checklist

☐ Understands general times of day, such as day and night.

☐ Knows own age and birthday.

☐ Understands position and spatial concepts, such as *up*, *down*, *full*, *empty*.

☐ Identifies simple opposites.

☐ Can sort items by color, shape, and size.

Write and Wipe Board Activities

Your child can use the write-and-wipe board located at the back of this book to practice writing skills and to further develop fine motor control. Giving your child many opportunities to color, write, and draw will help your child develop confidence in his or her beginning writing skills.

At first, your child should be given opportunities to use the write-and-wipe board just to scribble. Children are amazed at what they can do with a dry erase marker and a write-and-wipe board. Give your child ample opportunities to explore this new activity. Then, introduce the next activity.

Doodle Music

This exploration stage is a fun time to introduce Doodle Music. Choose a group of songs with distinct rhythms and tempos. For example, you might choose an upbeat children's song, a lullaby, marching music, and dance music. Tell your child to doodle while the music is playing. Play a portion of each type of music, changing the song about every 20 seconds or so. When the music tempo is fast, your child might color quickly. When the music slows, your child might color more slowly.

Scribble Chasing

Another fun activity is Scribble Chasing. You will need two dry erase markers for this activity. The first person draws a path on the board for the second person to follow. Continue creating paths and chasing until the board is completely covered with scribbles. Swap places and play again. This game can also be played using more controlled line drawing. For example, the first person draws short, straight lines for the second person to follow. The game can continue with horizontal, vertical, and diagonal line drawing.

Tracing Activities

Write your child's name or the individual letters of his or her name so he or she can trace over them. You can also draw circles, squares, or triangles for your child to trace. Remind your child that his or her drawing doesn't have to look exactly like your drawing.

Side-By-Side Drawing

In Side-By-Side Drawing, you draw a shape or a line and your child tries to draw a copy next to the original drawing. Vertical lines, horizontal lines, diagonal lines, and simple shapes are the best drawings to use with a beginner.

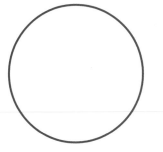
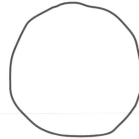

Do-It-Yourself Dot-to-Dots

Have your child draw several dots on the board. Encourage your child to draw lines between the dots until they are all connected. Have your child take a look at his or her creation to see if he or she can see a picture.

Tic-tac-toe

Play a fun game of Tic-tac-toe! Work with your child to draw a tic-tac-toe board. Then, use the game to practice writing letters. Start with the classic "X's" and "O's," then use different letters or shapes.

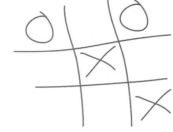

Tally Marks

Your child can use the board to keep track of the number of cars that drive by the window, the number of birds he or she hears chirping outside, or the number of stuffed animals he or she has. Model how you make a tally to keep track of a specific event. Depending on your child's age, you can teach him or her how to make a diagonal line to represent the 5th tally mark.

Phone Number Practice

It is never too early for your child to start learning his or her phone number. Write it on the write-and-wipe board. Have your child practice tracing over it or writing it underneath the number you wrote.

I Can Paste!

successfully completed the *Big Skills for Little Hands* book, *I Can Paste!*

_____
(name)

_____
(parent signature)

_____
(date)